A PRAYER WORKBOOK

PRAYER:
A DIVINE INVITATION

PASTOR CURTIS T. HALL

WESTBOW
PRESS®
A DIVISION OF THOMAS NELSON
& ZONDERVAN

WestBow Press books may be ordered through booksellers or by contacting:

WestBow Press
A Division of Thomas Nelson & Zondervan
1663 Liberty Drive
Bloomington, IN 47403
www.westbowpress.com
844-714-3454

Scripture taken from the King James Version of the Bible.

ISBN: 979-8-3850-1757-7 (sc)
ISBN: 979-8-3850-1758-4 (e)

Print information available on the last page.

WestBow Press rev. date: 01/23/2024

CONTENTS

CHAPTER 1

PRAYER

"And he spake a parable unto them to this end, that men ought to pray, and not to faint" Luke 18:1.

"Pray without ceasing" 1 Thessalonians 5:17.

You are probably wondering "why write another prayer workbook when there are a plethora of books and workbooks already available to be read and used?" Why even attempt to do something that has already been done? Well, the answer is simple. God has instituted prayer for our salvation and our well-being!

We were created in the image and likeness of God. The question is "How can we have His likeness and His image if we are not connected with Him?" It is having a relationship with God! Where we commune with Him about the affairs of life. It's about a "*love*" relationship with Him! "It is crucial for us to understand that the relationship of love that God established with mankind is not separate from His purpose God has for mankind."[1]

That intimate relationship with Christ helps us to get to know Him and His will for our lives! It is a means whereby God's will can be done on earth as it is in heaven. Prayer is nothing more than communion with God where you surrender your all to Him. It's revealing your most inner thoughts and feelings to the Creator of the universe. Prayer is something that every Christian should do and ought to do! Prayer should be given our highest priority! It's something that is commanded by God; "that men ought to pray, and not to faint" Luke 18:1.

We must understand that prayer is vital to our spiritual growth! It is just as important as breathing is to our existence! If we refuse or stop breathing, life would cease to exist. It is the same way with prayer. If we refuse or stop, our spiritual life will cease to exist! It is just that simple! Prayer is life! "Prayer is the life of the soul, the foundation of spiritual growth."[2]

Furthermore, Jesus gave us an example when it comes to prayer. You would find Him praying for Himself, His disciples and for believers. Prayer was His life! "Prayer was the secret of His

---

[1] Dr. Myles Munroe, *"Understanding the Purpose and Power of Prayer"* (New Kensington, PA: Whitaker House, 2002), p. 37

[2] Ellen White, *Prayer,*(Pacific Press Publishing Association, Nampa, ID, 2002), p.20

power, the law of His life, the inspiration of His toil and the source of His wealth, His joy, His communion and His strength."[3]

Prayer is something that a person can do anywhere, any place and any time, because there are no restraints with it. There's no limit to the amount of praying that a person can do!

Prayer is an invitation that Christ gives to each of us that we can come into His presence. We do not need an earthly priest to approach the King of the universe. The writer of Hebrews says it this way, "Let us therefore come [**boldly**] unto the throne of grace" Hebrews 4:16. We do not have to be afraid, ashamed, fearful, anxious, troubled or embarrassed to come before our Lord. We come to Him just as we are with all of our cares, concerns and burdens and can place them at His feet. Christ says in Matthew 11:28-30,

> "Come unto me, all *ye* that labour and are heavy laden, and I will give you rest.
> Take my yoke upon you, and learn of me; for I am meek and lowly in heart: and
> ye shall find rest unto your souls. For my yoke *is* easy, and my burden is light."

When we take His yoke upon us, we have the peace and rest that our hearts so desire! The peace that only Jesus can give! He says in John 14:27,

> "Peace I leave with you, my peace I give unto you: not as the world giveth, give I
> unto you. Let not your heart be troubled, neither let it be afraid."

Prayer lets us know that we have Someone who listens to our supplications and answers them according to His will! Prayer is "***personal and intentional***."

"The more we truly realize God's love for us, the more intimate our relationship will be with Him. The more intimate our relationship is with Him, the more meaningful our prayer lives will be."[4]

Prayer is its own reward. "Our intimate fellowship in prayer with Jesus pervades our lives of prosperity as well as adversity. It becomes its own reward, for the greatest blessing in prayer is communion with Jesus."[5] Just being in His presence should bring joy to the heart of the one praying. The more time we spend in the presence of Jesus, the closer we'll become more like Him. One fact that cannot be overlooked, Jesus loves to be in our company. He loves to hear our prayers and He gives us confidence and the assurance that our prayers will be answered! "In His loving embrace we lack absolutely no good thing. Like a flower that welcomes the morning sun, with confidence we open our lives to Him at the breaking of every day, believing that He will work out His perfect will for us."[6]

Prayer allows us to feel the love that Jesus has for us. It draws us into His presence where we can find peace, joy and contentment. "We have a nearness to Him and can hold sweet communion

---

[3] Alvin VanderGriend, *Praying God's Heart*, (PrayerShop Publishing, Terre Haute, IN, 2010), p. 24

[4] Dennis Smith, *Spirit Baptism and Prayer*, (Tyndale House Publishers, Inc., 2008), p. 6

[5] Philip Samaan, *Christ's Way To Pray*, (Review and Herald Publishing Association, Hagerstown, MD, 2006), p.26

[6] *Ibid*, p.26

with Him. We obtain distinct views of His tenderness and compassion and our hearts are broken and melted with contemplation of the love that is given to us."[7] The reward of prayer, knowing that I can come into His presence with all my faults, failures and short-comings and He'll accept me just as I am! Praise God!

---

[7] Ellen White, *Prayer,*(Pacific Press Publishing Association, Nampa, ID, 2002), p.11

1.) Read Luke 11:5-13; 18:1-8. In these verses, Jesus was speaking a parable on prayer. What point was He making in these verses concerning prayer?

_____

_____

2.) When Jesus spoke about the widow and the friend, how does it illustrate the point on prayer?

_____

_____

3.) What do these passages teach us about God?

_____

_____

4.) In Luke 11:9 and Luke 18:1, 8, the Lord is calling for us to have what kind of attitude?

_____

_____

5.) Why does God want us to ask Him for things when He already knows our needs?

_____

_____

6.) According to these verses, can God's attitude have an effect on our prayers? Explain your answers.

_____

_____

7.) How has these verses influenced you on the attitude of prayer? If so, why?

_____

_____

8.) What does prayer mean to you and your relationship with Jesus?

_____

_____

CHAPTER 2

WHAT IS PRAYER?

"I will therefore that men pray every where, lifting up holy hands, without wrath and doubting" 1 Timothy 2:8.

"Be careful for nothing; but in every thing by prayer and supplication with thanksgiving let your requests be made known unto God" Philippians 4:6.

We are admonished to pray so that we can be in communion with the Lord, making our requests and supplications known to Him. However, we must realize that prayer is more than just asking the Lord for something in our lives. It's allowing Jesus to come into our hearts, where He can abide in us. The apostle John writes in John 15:7,

"If ye abide in me, and my words abide in you, ye shall ask what ye will, and it shall be done unto you."

In order for our prayers to be answered, we must have the divine nature of Christ dwelling within. Our thoughts aims, ambitions, desires and dreams are to be in Christ and in accordance to His will! When our prayers ascend up to God, He hears them and gives the answers that best suits each individuals.

The question is asked, "What is prayer?" The answer can be as simple as communion with God. Talking with Him as a friend to a friend. Prayer is just having a conversation with the King of the universe. It's developing a relationship with God! In order to strengthen this relationship, we spend time with Him and read and study His word. Tell Him what's on our minds. From the book *Steps to Christ*, the author writes that "prayer is the opening of the heart to God as to a friend. Not that it is necessary in order to make known to God what we are, but in order to enable us to receive Him. Prayer does not bring God down to us, but brings us up to Him."[8]

We don't have to use big and elaborate words to express our feelings or to tell God what's in our hearts. All we need to do is just talk with Him. Tell Him the things that are troubling or that are burdens. Cheryl Sacks defines prayer as

"Prayer is communion with the living God. Without prayer, the life flow from Christ to His

---

[8] Ellen White, *Prayer,*(Pacific Press Publishing Association, Nampa, ID, 2002), p. 93

body is cut off; the church ceases to be a living organism and becomes little different from any other organization."[9] It's about the attitude that we have concerning prayer! "If we can change our attitude toward prayer – thinking of it as a process that builds our relationship with God – and cultivate a daily prayer time, we can become strong people of prayer. And the prayer life we develop has the potential to completely transform our lives."[10]

Prayer is not a duty, but a privilege and a necessity! We must realize that prayer is needed more now than ever before in earth's history! It is the line that He uses to touch the hearts of the people! God initiated prayer between Him and man.

Ellen White writes that "prayer is the breath of the soul. It is the secret of spiritual power. No other means of grace can be substituted and the health of the soul be preserved."[11]

Prayer is having a personal relationship with God and He responds to us in a personal way. It's personal to Him as well! He responds to each individual differently based upon their needs. A person doesn't have to be educated, or have status, or wealth, or great possessions to approach God in prayer. The only thing that's needed is a willing heart and desire to serve God! "Our eternal life depends on knowing God. A meaningful prayer life is essential for us to know God as we must if we are to be among the redeemed when He comes."[12] This may sound repetitive, "the heart of prayer is communion with God in a unity of love and purpose. It is agreeing with God – heart – soul – mind, and strength – to bring about God's will."[13]

However, we must understand that just because we pray in the name of Jesus doesn't mean that all our prayers will be answered the way that we want!

There is no magical formula or guarantee that our prayers will be answered! It's about what the name stands for. It's about knowing God and His will for our lives! "We're not effective in prayer just by using the word Jesus, but in understanding the significance of who He really is and appropriating His power through faith in His name."[14]

---

[9] Cheryl Sacks, *The Prayer Saturated Church*, (Navpress, Colorado Springs, CO, 2004), p. 28.

[10] John Maxwell, *Partners in Prayer*, (Nelson Books Publishers, Nashville, TN, 1996), p. 16

[11] Ellen White, *Prayer*,(Pacific Press Publishing Association, Nampa, ID, 2002), p.12

[12] Dennis Smith, *Spirit Baptism and Prayer*, (Tyndale House Publishers, Inc., 2008), p. 7

[13] Dr. Myles Munroe, *"Understanding the Purpose and Power of Prayer"* (New Kensington, PA: Whitaker House, 2002), p. 41

[14] *Ibid*, p.231

QUESTIONS FOR REFLECTION:

1.) How would you define prayer?

_____

_____

2.) How is the relationship between God and you developed?

_____

_____

3.) Why is prayer so important in the life?

_____

_____

4.) If my attitude towards prayer is indifferent, how will it affect my prayer life?

_____

_____

5.) Can you identify anyone from Scripture that had a bad or indifferent attitude when they prayed?

_____

_____

6.) A meaningful prayer life is _____ for us to _____ _____ as we must if we are

to be _____ the _____ when He _____.

CHAPTER 3

WHY PRAY?

"And he spake a parable unto them to this end, that men ought always to pray, and not to faint;" Luke 18:1.

"Praying always with all prayer and supplication in the Spirit, and watching thereunto with all perseverance and supplication for all saints;" Ephesians 6:18.

"Pray without ceasing." 1 Thessalonians 5:17.

Jesus says in the text above "that men ought always to pray and not to faint." So that gives us an indication why we should pray! It was commanded by God! The apostle Paul says that we should pray always and to be continuous in prayer. Praying is important for our soul salvation and eternal life! Prayer was vital to the life of our Savior! He found enjoyment when He was communing with His Father! He received power and strength when He prayed! Jesus spent entire nights in prayer.

Prayer brings us in the presence of God, where we draw strength and power. It builds us up spiritually and connects us with God Himself. For those reasons alone is why we should pray!

"Prayer "is an expression of submission to God and dependence upon Him"[15] and Him alone. Our dependence should not be on anyone else, because they cannot handle the stresses of every day life! Only God can! He knows how to handle our cares, concerns and burdens. The apostle Peter says that we should cast our care (burdens) upon Him. 1 Peter 5:7.

Why pray? Because it allows God to accomplish that which He would not accomplish without our prayers. In other words, if we did not pray, God cannot do all that He wants to do! Through prayer, we give Him permission and authority to save those that are in darkness!

God has voluntarily made Himself dependent upon our prayers. The church received power to rule the world through our prayers. Through our prayers, God acts and speaks.

Why pray? Because our salvation and the salvation of others are dependent upon our prayer! "Prayer is necessary because from the beginning God intended to work through humans and not independently of them, in completing His will on earth. God works through the prayers of His people."[16]

---

[15] H. B. Charles, JR., *It Happens After Prayer*, (Moody publishers, Chicago, IL, 2013), p. 16

[16] Dennis Smith, *Spirit Baptism and Prayer*, (Tyndale House Publishers, Inc., 2008), p. 11

"God needs our prayers to aid in His work, not because He is not powerful enough without us, but because He has voluntarily limited Himself to allow humanity to participate in the salvation of the world. This is part of His eternal plan."[17]

The Bible says in Matthew 6:10, "Thy will be done in earth, as *it is* in heaven." God wants His will be to done on earth as it is in heaven. He wants to save as many people as He can and He wants our prayers to assist Him in saving others! "Satan knows that if he can get the Christian to be negligent in the area of prayer, he has little to fear concerning the believer's spiritual growth in Christ or his effectiveness as a laborer for God in His work on earth."[18]

Why pray? Because we need Jesus in our lives! He can cleanse us from all sin and defilement. We can pray the prayer that David prayed in Psalm 51. However, there are times when we feel too embarrassed or too ashamed to approach Him in prayer! But that is the time to approach Him! That is our greatest need to be forgiven and accepted by Jesus! One writer writes, "The more needy, the more qualified. He looks beyond our faults and sees our need; He specifically invites the weary and heavy laden to come to Him."[19] "God often brings people to a crisis to show them their own weakness and to point them to the Source of strength. If they pray and watch unto prayer, fighting bravely, their weak points will become their strong points."[20]

That's why prayer should be focused upon God and our love for Him. Why prayer? Cheryl Sacks affirms;

"Because it is right Luke 18:1.

Because it is commanded 1 Thessalonians 5:17.

Because it is sinful to neglect 1 Samuel 12:23.

Because neglect of it grieves God Isaiah 43:21-22.

Because it is the medium through which God bestows blessing Matthew 7:11; Daniel 9:3.

Because it is essential to victory over the forces of evil Ephesians 6:12-18.

Because of the obligation imposed by Christ's example Hebrews 5:7.

Because of the emphasis given to it in the early church Acts 2:42; 6:4; 12:5."[21]

Why pray? To have an intimate relationship with our Lord and Savior Jesus Christ!

---

[17] Carrol J. Shewmaker, *When We Pray For Others*, (Review & Harold Publishing, Hagerstown, MD, 1995), p. 20, 21

[18] Dennis Smith, *Spirit Baptism and Prayer*, (Tyndale House Publishers, Inc., 2008), p. 10

[19] Philip Samaan, *Christ's Way To Pray*, (Review and Herald Publishing Association, Hagerstown, MD, 2006), p.73,

[20] Ellen White, *Christ Triumphant*, (Review and Herald Publishing Association, Hagerstown, MD, 1999) p. 89

[21] Cheryl Sacks, *The Prayer Saturated Church*, (NavPress, Colorado Springs, CO 80935, 2004), p. 23

1.) What does prayer do to our spiritual lives?

_____(It builds us up spiritually and connects us with God Himself) _____

_____

2.) Our _____ should not be on _____ because they cannot _____

the stresses of _____ _____ _____.

3.) If we did not pray, would God carry on His work of salvation?

_____

_____

4.) What do our prayers accomplish in the life of the unbeliever?

_____

_____

5.) How would you categorize your prayer life right now?

    a.) Boring
    b.) Exciting
    c.) Dry
    d.) Powerful
    e.) Tasking
    f.) Mechanical
    g.) Effective

6.) List at least three reasons why we need to pray?

_____

_____

CHAPTER 4

THE NEGLECT OF PRAYER

"And he spake a parable unto them to this end, that men ought always to pray, and not to faint;" Luke 18:1.

Prayer is a necessity that keeps us connected to the source of power. Prayer keeps our hearts and minds focused on Jesus. However, the neglect of prayer causes our spirituality to become weak and feeble. It appears prayer is not given priority in the life of believers. "What a wonder it is that we pray so little. God is ready and willing to hear the sincere prayer of the humblest of His children and yet there is much manifest reluctance on our part to make known our wants to God."[22]

When it comes to prayer, nothing should stand in between you and your Savior! This is a sacred time that's devoted to God and God alone. The proverbial saying, "much prayer, much power; little prayer, little power; no prayer, no power." There is power in prayer! But if believers do not take full advantage of the privilege of prayer, it does them no good! Plus, we can grieve the Spirit of God when we don't pray! How can we receive power when we don't pray? It's impossible! The only way to stay power connected is to pray!

However, the neglect of prayer will cause the powers of darkness to prevail over the hearts of men. Satan will try to use his powers of deception and manipulate the minds of men! When prayer is neglected, we lose that wholeness that we have with God. We lose the experience of being in His presence and allowing His Spirit to fill our hearts! Ellen White writes, "neglect the exercise of prayer, or engage in prayer spasmodically, now and then, as seems convenient and you lose your hold on God. The spiritual faculties lose their vitality, the religious experience lacks health and vigor."[23] It is vitally important that we do not neglect prayer! If ever there was a source of power, it is prayer!

I wish I could tell you the importance of prayer in the life! Thus far, in this book, we have been discussing why prayer is so necessary and the importance of it. If we lose that concept and begin to neglect prayer, then our spiritual lives will wane and become weak!

The above text and 1 Thessalonians 5:17 "pray without ceasing" is talking about prayer as a way of life. Something that should be done as part of our lives! We should wake up in the morning and pray. Noon day, we should pray. At evening time, pray! It's just a way of life! Prayer

---

[22] Ellen White, *Prayer,*(Pacific Press Publishing Association, Nampa, ID, 2002), p.24

[23] *Ibid,* p. 13

is a necessity! Why? Because of "the temptations to which we are daily exposed make prayer a necessity. In order that we may be kept by the power of God through faith, the desires of the mind should be continually ascending in silent prayer for help, for light, for strength, for knowledge. But thought and prayer cannot take the place of earnest, faithful improvement of the time. Work and prayer are both in perfecting Christian character."[24]

That's why Christians should never neglect to pray! If we do nothing else, we can pray! Pray for strength, power and the Holy Spirit to fill our lives! Read Matthew 26:36-46 of the disciples in the Garden of Gethsemane and how they neglected to pray for Christ in His most critical hour! Instead of praying, they all were asleep! This is what Ellen White writes about this in her book *Desire of Ages,*

> "Rising with painful effort, He staggered to the place where He had left His companions. But He "findeth them asleep." Had He found them praying, He would have been relieved. Had they been seeking refuge in God, that satanic agencies might not prevail over them, He would have been comforted by their steadfast faith. But they had not heeded the repeated warning, "Watch and pray.". . They did not intend to forsake their Lord, but they seemed paralyzed by a stupor which they might have shaken off if they had continued pleading with God. They did not realize the necessity of watchfulness and earnest prayer in order to withstand temptation."[25]

To neglect prayer is a detrimental to our spiritual being! We must heed the warnings that Jesus gave us to "watch, pray and be ready." To neglect to pray could cost us our eternity!

[24] *Ibid*, p. 25
[25] Ellen White, *Desire of Ages*, (Pacific Press Publishing Association, Nampa, Idaho, 2005), p. 688

1.) Why is prayer a necessity and a duty?

_____

_____

2.) Can we grieve the Holy Spirit by neglecting to prayer?

_____

_____

3.) What else occurs when we neglect to pray?

_____

_____

4.) Neglect the _____ of prayer, or _____ in _____,

now and then, as seems _____ and you lose your _____ on _____.

5.) What are some advantages of not neglecting to pray?

_____

_____

6.) Once again, read the account of the disciples in Matthew 26:36-46. List reasons why you think the disciples went to sleep and did not pray.

_____

_____

CHAPTER 5

PRAY IN JESUS' NAME

"And whatsoever ye shall ask in my name, that will I do, that the Father may be glorified in the Son. If ye shall ask any thing in my name, I will do it" John 14:13-14.

To pray in Jesus' name is with reverence, awe and respect. His name is holy and should be treated as such. When angels speak that name, they veil their faces and bow in holy reverence. Jesus is given the honor, reverence and glory due to His name! Never should His name be dishonored or disrespected. God is Creator of all things and He alone deserves our reverence and admiration. Individuals speaking Jesus name should bow in total reverence. The psalmist declares, "God is greatly to be feared in the assembly of the saints and to be had in reverence of all them that are about Him" Psalm 89:7. "He sent redemption unto his people: he hath commanded his covenant forever: holy and reverend *is* his name" Psalm 111:9.

When we pray in Jesus' name, we align our wills with His will that His will might be done on earth. We are one with Him in thoughts, deeds and actions. From the book, Desire of Ages, Ellen White writes, "All true obedience comes from the heart. It was heart work with Christ. And if we consent, He will so identify Himself with our thoughts and aims, so blend our hearts and minds into conformity to His will, that when obeying Him we shall be but carrying out our own impulses. The will, refined and sanctified, will find its highest delight in doing His service. When we know God as it is our privilege to know Him, our life will be a life of continual obedience. Through an appreciation of the character of Christ, through communion with God, sin will become hateful to us."[26]

This kind of praying places you at the throne room of God. Our petitions will reflect the love and authority of Jesus. When we pray in Jesus' name, we have all authority – authority over the enemy and everything that he tries to do! There's power in His name and we are given the promise that "No weapon that is formed against thee shall prosper" Isaiah 54:17.

"When we truly want what God wants and turn such desires into prayer, those prayers will be prayers in Jesus' name. When the Spirit of truth lives in us and makes God's will known to us, we will pray in Jesus' name."[27] It is more than just asking for our will to be done, but to connect our will with His will.

---

[26] Ellen White, *Desire of Ages*, (Pacific Press Publishing Association, Nampa, Idaho, 2005), p. 688
[27] Alvin VanderGriend, *Praying God's Heart*, (PrayerShop Publishing, Terre Haute, IN, 2010), p. 16

Praying in Jesus' name will heighten our religious experience, because we are doing what the Lord has asked of us! We are making His desires our desires so that His work can be done on earth. Our prayers will be mixed with His prayers as they go before the Father. "The prayer of the humble suppliant He presents as His own desire in that soul's behalf. Every sincere prayer is heard in heaven. It may not be fluently expressed; but if the heart is in it, it will ascend to the sanctuary where Jesus ministers, and He will present it to the Father without one awkward, stammering word, beautiful and fragrant with the incense of His own perfection."[28]

My words may not be eloquent or fancy, but as long as I'm sincere, God hears my prayers! Why? Because Jesus takes my words and presents them to the Father without any mistakes in them! My prayers will be answered because Jesus is interceding for me! Praise God!

"Christ is the connecting link between God and man. He has promised His personal intercession. He places the whole virtue of His righteousness on the side of the suppliant. He pleads for man, and man, in need of divine help, pleads for himself in the presence of God, using the influence of the One who gave His life for the life of the world."[29] It is truly a blessing when we can pray in Jesus' name.

"When we pray in Jesus' name, through His blood, we use our position of authority in Christ to make known to demonic rulers the perfect will of God. This is something that only we in the church can do. There is no one else who can change the spiritual climate over communities, who can open the door for people to respond to the gospel."[30]

---

[28] Ellen White, *Desire of Ages*, (Pacific Press Publishing Association, Nampa, Idaho, 2005), p. 687
[29] Ellen White, *Testimonies for the Church, vol. 8*, (Pacific Press Publishing Association, Boise, Idaho, 1948), p. 178
[30] Cheryl Sacks, *The Prayer Saturated Church*, (NavPress, Colorado Springs, CO 80935, 2004), p. 205

1.) What does it mean to pray in Jesus' name?

_____

_____

2.) Several things occur when we pray in Jesus' name. List some of them.

_____

_____

3.) When we _____ God as it is _____ _____ to know _____, our _____ will

be a _____ of _____ _____.

4.) What will our petitions do for us when we pray in Jesus' name?

_____

_____

5.) Explain how praying in Jesus' name can change you as a person. Or does it?

_____

_____

6.) When we pray in Jesus' name do we use our authority over the enemy and his forces? True or False. Explain your answer.

_____

_____

CHAPTER 6

THE HOLY SPIRIT AND PRAYER

"Likewise the Spirit also helpeth our infirmities: for we know not what we should pray for as we ought: but the Spirit itself maketh intercession for us with groanings which cannot be uttered" Romans 8:26

The Holy Spirit, the Third person of the Godhead is promised to every believer who ask for Him. The Bible says that God is more willing to give us the Holy Spirit than parents are willing to give good gifts to their children. Luke 11:13. He is the One that inspires us to pray and brings us into connection with God. The Holy Spirit empowers our prayers and gives us the desire and passion to witness.

However, in order to receive the Holy Spirit, we must empty ourselves of self! We must allow Him to have complete control of our hearts, minds and souls. Before the Holy Spirit was given, the disciples had to come together and repent and confess their sins so that they might be worthy vessels to do the work of the Lord! They emptied themselves so that they might be filled with the Spirit of God. From the book, *The Acts of the Apostles*, Ellen White writes,

> "The disciples prayed with intense earnestness for a fitness to meet men and in their daily intercourse to speak words that would lead sinners to Christ. Putting away all differences, all desire for the supremacy, they came close together in Christian fellowship. They drew nearer and nearer to God, and as they did this they realized what a privilege had been theirs in being permitted to associate so closely with Christ."[31]

Once we have the Holy Spirit in our lives, we have the life of Christ in us. "The Holy Spirit is the breath of spiritual life in the soul. The impartation of the Spirit is the impartation of the life of Christ. It imbues the receiver with the attributes of Christ."[32]

The Spirit of God plays an important role in our prayer life. He directs our prayers, He inspires us and tells us what we should pray for. He is the One that leads, guides and directs. "When we are praying in the Spirit, our prayers will be empowered by the Spirit. Our prayers will be effective

---

[31] Ellen White, *Acts of the Apostles*, (Pacific Press Publishing Association, 2005), p. 37
[32] Ellen White, *Desires of Ages*, (Pacific Press Publishing Association, Nampa, ID, 2002), p.805

and bring powerful results."[33] The answers that we seek when we pray will come because we are praying in the Spirit of God. Self is forgotten and we are caught up in the throne room of heaven making our petitions and supplications known unto God! This kind of praying "moves the arms of God, move His arms to destroy works of the devil. Satan can deal with most everything we come at him with, but he cannot deal with the arm of the Lord moved through prayer."[34]

Even though God is willing to pour out His Holy Spirit upon His people, the church has not relied upon the power that God wants to freely give. "We have learned to depend on our own wisdom, instead of God's wisdom. We depend on our methods, plans and strategies to advance God's work. We use our management and training skills to manage the daily operations of the church. We also look to psychological insights in order to deal with people rather than insights of the Spirit."[35] Using all those things are good in themselves, but to receive power from above, we need the Holy Spirit in our lives! We must seek the infilling of the Spirit each and every day! It is not a one-time thing! The apostle Paul writes, "Be filled with the Spirit" Ephesians 5:18. "For which cause we faint not; but though our outward man perish, yet the inward man is renewed day by day" 2 Corinthians 4:16.

When we are filled with the Holy Spirit, our lives will come into conformity with the will of God. No longer will our prayers be of a selfish or self-centered, but will be Christ-centered. Our hearts will be transformed by the power of the Spirit! "When the Spirit of God takes possession of the heart, it transforms the life. Sinful thoughts are put away, evil deeds are renounced; love, humility, and peace take the place of anger, envy, and strife. Joy takes the place of sadness, and the countenance reflects the light of heaven."[36] Everything about us will change, because we will reflect the love of God in our hearts!

The Bible declares in Acts 1:14, "These all continued with one accord in prayer and supplication." While the disciples were waiting for the outpouring of the Holy Spirit, one thing occupied their minds and it was hope for the future. "And they were steadfast in prayer. The Holy Spirit came at a prayer meeting. Heart beat with heart and prayer mingled with prayer. And every recorded instance of receiving the Holy Spirit in the New Testament is preceded by earnest prayer."[37]

[33] Dennis Smith, *Spirit Baptism and Prayer*, (Tyndale House Publishers, Inc., 2008), p. 28
[34] Alvin VanderGriend, *Praying God's Heart*, (PrayerShop Publishing, Terre Haute, IN, 2010), p. 126, 127
[35] Dennis Smith, *Spirit Baptism and Prayer*, (Tyndale House Publishers, Inc., 2008), p. 25
[36] Ellen White, *Desires of Ages*, (Pacific Press Publishing Association, Nampa, ID, 2002), p. 173
[37] Leroy Froom, *Coming of the Comforter*, (Review & Herald, Hagerstown, MD, 1956), p. 109

1.) In order to receive the Holy Spirit in our lives, what must we do first?

_____

_____

2.) When we pray, how will our answers come?

_____

_____

3.) Before the Holy Spirit was _____, the _____ had to _____ _____ and

_____ and _____ their sins so that they _____ be _____

to do the _____ of the Lord!

4.) How important a role does the Holy Spirit play in our lives?

_____

_____

5.) _____ can _____ with most _____ we _____ at him with, but

_____ _____ deal with the _____ of the _____ _____

through _____.

6.) The Holy Spirit was given so that He could accomplish the work that God wanted Him to do through us. However, instead of relying upon Him, what has the church relied upon?

_____

_____

CHAPTER 7

TYPES OF PRAYERS

"And he spake a parable unto them to this end, that men ought always to pray, and not to faint;" Luke 18:1

Praying seems so simple and yet so profound. We know that prayer takes us into the throne room of our heavenly Father. We say whatever comes to our minds at the time we pray. Most of the time it is without a form or pattern. We start our prayer and then conclude it. However, the Bible informs us that there is a certain way to pray. It has a beginning, middle and conclusion. Often our prayers begin with stating the things that we desire and crave. Praying this way can lead to selfish prayers, centering on self and not on Christ! From the book, praying God's Heart, the author writes, "One of the strangest things about prayer is that it can be the most selfish activity in the world. Prayer can be merely seeking to use God for one's own purpose."[38]

However, prayer has a style that first focuses upon God and exalts Him above anything or anyone. It is first giving Him the honor and glory that He deserves. Recognizing Him for who He is and what He means to you and then move on in your prayers! So we want to explore the different types of prayers.

First, using the acronym ACTS, which has four basic parts of the prayer: adoration, confession, thanksgiving and supplication. "Adoration lifts us out of ourselves to behold the wonder and beauty of God."[39] It's honoring and giving all the glory to God Himself and not to another. The psalmist writes,

> "I will extol thee, my God, O king; and I will bless thy name for ever and ever. Every day will I bless thee; and I will praise thy name for ever and ever. Great *is* the LORD, and greatly to be praised; and his greatness *is* unsearchable" Psalm 145:1-3.

Another way of showing adoration in our prayers is by praising God. God rejoices in our praise. We praise God for being who He is and honoring Him for all that He has done! We worship God and praise His name. Psalm 34:1,

---

[38] Alvin VanderGriend, *Praying God's Heart*, (PrayerShop Publishing, Terre Haute, IN, 2010), p. 126, 37
[39] Greg Ogden, *Discipleship Essentials*, (IVP Connect, Downers Grove, Illinois, 2007), p.49

"I will bless the LORD at all times: his praise *shall* continually *be* in my mouth."

Psalm 100:4,

"Enter into his gates with thanksgiving, *and* into his courts with praise: be thankful unto him, *and* bless his name."

"Why does God want us to praise Him? Not only because He deserves it, but for what we get out of it. What is the greatest thing God can give us? More of Himself. Praise is the sweet echo of his own excellence in the hearts of His people."[40] We need to start our prayers with praise and exalting God throughout it. Tell Him what He means to you. We can say things like "Father, You are the Creator and Redeemer of earth and the Maker of all things." Describes His goodness and mercy towards you. The entire prayer is focused upon God!

The next step is confession. This is where in the prayer we confess our sins and short-comings. We don't want to start our prayers without confessing our sins! We see our unrighteousness and our unworthiness and fall at the feet of Jesus. The Bible reassures us that if we confess our sins, God will forgive us and cleanse us! 1 John 1:9. "By making confession a regular part of our conversation with the Lord, we are giving Him permission to show us our lives through His eyes."[41]

When David confessed his sins, it was with true repentance and a contrite heart. He says in Psalm 51:1-4,

"Have mercy upon me, O God, according to thy lovingkindness: according unto the multitude of thy tender mercies blot out my transgressions. Wash me thoroughly from mine iniquity, and cleanse me from my sin. For I acknowledge my transgressions: and my sin is ever before me.

"Against thee, thee only, have I sinned, and done this evil in thy sight: that thou mightest be justified when thou speakest, and be clear when thou judgest."

We must also understand that confession is imperative in our relationship with the Lord! It shows that we are relying upon Him for our strength and power. It shows that we want all of our iniquities to be blotted out before God!

However, there's another part to forgiveness in our prayers! As we ask God for forgiveness, we must also forgive others who have sinned against us! It is imperative that we do. Jesus says in Matthew 6:15, "But if ye forgive not men their trespasses, neither will your Father forgive your trespasses." "Nothing can justify an unforgiving spirit. He who is unmerciful toward others shows that he himself is not a partaker of God's pardoning grace."[42]

---

[40] *Ibid*, p.50
[41] *Ibid*, p.50
[42] Ellen White, *Christ's Object Lessons*,((Pacific Press Publishing Association, Washington, D. C., 1941), p. 251

Next there's thanksgiving, giving thanks for what God has done for us. Thank Him for life, health, strength, our homes, and the ability to move and have our being. Ephesians 5:20 declares,

> "Giving thanks always for all things unto God and the Father in the name of our
> Lord Jesus Christ;"

All that we are doing is just thanking God for all that He has done for us. It's showing our gratitude towards Him. "We so easily lose our sense of gratitude and forget the good things the Lord has done for us. Thanksgiving is the cultivation of a memory. It is prayerfully listing the good that is in our life."[43]

Then there's supplication where we place our petitions at Jesus' feet. In earnest and perseverance, we plead with Him. This is where we use the "A.S.K" formula: ask, seek and find, which is recorded in Matthew 7:7. Ephesians 6:18 states, "Praying always with all prayer and supplication in the Spirit, and watching thereunto with all perseverance and supplication for all saints;" We do not give up in prayer. We stay on our knees until the answer comes! "God does not say, 'ask once and you shall receive. He bids us ask. Unwearyingly persist in prayer.

The persistent asking brings the petitioner into a more earnest attitude and gives him an increase desire to receive the things for which he asks."[44]

"Our prayers are to be as earnest and persistent as was the petition of the needy friend who asked for the loaves at midnight. The more earnestly and steadfastly we ask, the closer will be our spiritual union with Christ. We shall receive increased blessings because we have increased faith."[45]

---

[43] Greg Ogden, *Discipleship Essentials*, (IVP Connect, Downers Grove, Illinois, 2007), p.51
[44] Ellen White, *Christ's Object Lessons*, (Pacific Press Publishing Association, Washington, D. C., 1941), p. 145
[45] *Ibid*, p. 146

1.) Does it really matter if I use a pattern when I pray?

_____

_____

2.) How is prayer self-centered and self-focused?

_____

_____

3.) One of the _____ things about _____ is that it can be the _____ _____ activity in the _____. _____ can be _____ _____ to _____ God for _____ _____ purpose."

4.) Why should we be thankful to God in prayer?

_____

_____

5.) What is the greatest thing that God can give us?

_____

_____

6.) Are your prayers more self-centered or God-centered? Think about the way you pray.

_____

_____

7.) Would you find it easy or difficult to use the ACTS method of prayer?

_____

_____

CHAPTER 8

TYPES OF PRAYERS PART – 2

"And he spake a parable unto them to this end, that men ought always to pray, and not to faint;" Luke 18:1

Elder Roy Rugles, a retired pastor presented a presentation on the Lord's Prayer. In his presentation, he used the acronym PCPCP style of prayer. Even though this is in the Lord's Prayer, it still gives us a method of praying. PCPCP is an acronym for prelude, consecration, petition, confession, protection and praise. The focus of this prayer is once again to place God first and exalt, praise and honor Him. This prayer recognizes God as the Sovereign of the universe and Creator of the universe. He alone is to be praised!

He begins his presentation with **prelude;**

P – Prelude:

I. Lift your mind heavenward – see the throne of God. Forget the mundane things of everyday life and focus your mind towards heaven where God reigns.

II. My Father – pause,
Think about what that means.

- Our relationship to Him and His love for us.
- Our relationship to one another. We're related – brothers and sisters.
- Our obligation to our heavenly Father as His children.

III. "Which art in heaven" – Pause
Think about His position and power.

IV. "Hallowed be thy name" – Pause

- Think about how holy He is and how we should approach Him with reverence and awe.
- Think about how we should be holy and live holy lives.
- **C – Consecration:**

V. "Thy kingdom come, Thy will be done"

1. Begin confessing your sins.
2. Ask for forgiveness.
3. Pray for help in overcoming certain sins.
4. Re-dedicate your life to Christ and ask Him to come into your heart.
5. Surrender the will – ask God to help you do so.
6. Ask Him to use you today in His service.

P - Petition

VI. "Give us this day"

1. Ask for spiritual bread to give to others.
2. Ask for physical things for yourself and others.
3. Claim a Bible promise with the request.

C – Confession

VII. "Forgive us our debts"

1. Ask for help in forgiving those who have wronged you.
2. Ask for God's love in your heart.

P – Protection and Praise:

VIII. "Lead us not"

1. Ask for God's guidance in your walk today and for Him to "keep you" from evil and for strength to overcome.

IX. "Thine is the kingdom"

1. Thank him for past blessings.
2. Thank God in advance for what He is going to do in answer to your prayer.
3. Praise Him.[46]

   "The Lord desires us to make mention of His goodness and tell of His power. He is honored by the expression of praise and thanksgiving."[47]

---

[46] Elder Roy Rugles, *Teach Us To Pray,* An Instructional Seminar on Prayer (Used by Permission)

[47] Ellen White, *Christ's Object Lessons,* (Pacific Press Publishing Association, Washington, D. C., 1941), p. 298

CHAPTER 9

THE LORD'S PRAYER

"After this manner therefore pray ye: Our Father which art in heaven, Hallowed be thy name. Thy kingdom come. Thy will be done in earth, as it is in heaven. Give us this day our daily bread. And forgive us our debts, as we forgive our debtors. And lead us not into temptation, but deliver us from evil: For thine is the kingdom, and the power, and the glory, for ever. Amen" Matthew 6:9-13.

The Lord's Prayer is one that many people, including children know and it is the most repeated prayer that's prayed. This prayer is a model that we should follow when we pray. Many people just repeat the words and really do not comprehend the meaning of them. When the Savior prayed this prayer, He was communing with His Father for strength, discernment, to know His Father's will. It was more than just sounding off words. Jesus was establishing a relationship with His Father. He relied upon His Father for strength and power to endure the trials of the day. This prayer is to bring us closer to the Father as we commune with Him. This prayer is about a relationship that we should have with God, the Father.

The disciples notice Jesus praying and were moved. These men knew how to pray, but there was something about the way that Jesus prayed! It stirred their souls as they heard Him pray. It seemed as though their prayers were just words resounding in the air. This prayer was a model for them to follow. It was a prayer that started with God and ended with God! The prayer was God-centered and God focused! So they asked Jesus to teach them how to pray.

Jesus' prayer was different from that of the religious leaders of His day. His words appeared to be reaching the throne room of God where He sits on His throne! His words had power and seemed to move mountains. His words were not vain repetitions as the Pharisees used in their praying. The disciples thought that if only they could pray as Jesus prayed, their own effectiveness as disciples would be greatly increased. There was power in His prayer.

As Jesus commenced in His prayer, He began with **"Our Father."** He first showed our relationship with Him. We are His sons and daughters in the family of God. "The fact that He is our Father binds us together as Christians in the great, universal fellowship of faith with men who in sincerity and truth recognize the Father of our Lord Jesus Christ."[48]

---

[48] Ellen White, *SDA Commentary* Vol. 5, (Review & Harold Publishing, Hagerstown, MD, 1956), p. 346

This is an endearing term which indicates His relationship with us and His tender concern and care for us. It gives us assurance, confidence and faith, when we approach the throne of God. We have been adopted into His family, made possible through Christ. He loves us as He loves His Son. 1 John 3:2 declares,

> "Beloved, now are we the sons of God, and it doth not yet appear what we shall be: but we know that, when he shall appear, we shall be like him; for we shall see him as he is."

Knowing that He loves us like a Father, gives us the confidence to approach the throne of grace and the faith that says "we know that when we pray, He hears us" 1 John 5:14.

Not only that, but when God is given His proper place, everything else will fall into place. We have a heavenly Father who cares for us immensely. He's anxious to hear our prayers. He is personal and sovereign. It combines two concepts: first, the fatherhood of God; as a loving, caring Father and secondly, the sovereignty of God. God's love is always driven by His power. And God's power is motivated by God's love.

> "Doubtless thou *art* our father, though Abraham be ignorant of us, and Israel acknowledge us not: thou, O LORD, *art* our father, our redeemer; thy name *is* from everlasting" Isaiah 63:16.

> "Like as a father pitieth *his* children, *so* the LORD pitieth them that fear him. For he knoweth our frame; he remembereth that we *are* dust" Psalm 103:13, 14.

From the book *Thoughts from Mount of Blessing*, Ellen White writes,

> "He hears every word that is spoken, listens to every prayer that is offered, tastes the sorrows and disappointments of every soul, regards the treatment that is given to father, mother, sister, friend, and neighbor.

> "He cares for our necessities, and His love and mercy and grace are continually flowing to satisfy our need"[49]

God loves us as He loves Jesus! We are not orphans, or street children begging for food. We're sons and daughters of God. He's our loving heavenly Father. Jesus is so eager to welcome us into the family of God. In Christ, we are one family with a Father who will guide us. A Father who will strengthen us. A Father who will sustain us. A Father who will empower us. A Father who will protect us. A Father who will provide for us.

"Which art in heaven" reminds us of the location and position of God. He is sovereign of the universe and the Creator of all things. It lets us know of God's power, greatness and His majesty. He is sovereign over the universe. He's in control of what takes place. He guides what

---

[49] Ellen White, *Thoughts From the Mount of Blessing*, (Pacific Press Publishing, Boise, Idaho), p. 105

takes place in our lives. He's the God of might, majesty and the God of power! He delights for us to come to Him in prayer.

"Our Father which art in heaven" brings together two profound concepts: the love of God and the power of God. The power of God is motivated by the love of God! The love of God is always backed by the power of God. As long as we know that the fact that God is in heaven, there's no need to fear or be discouraged, because we have a heavenly Father that cares for us! There's no need to worry, or feel despondent. Why? Because God is there ready to take care of all our problems, frustrations and concerns. We can say as did the psalmist when he said "What time I am afraid, I will trust in Thee" Psalm 56:3. The One that loves us the most has the power to change any hopeless situation. Here's a statement that should bring joy into our hearts.

Ellen White writes,

> "God calls upon His faithful ones, who believe in Him, to talk courage to those who are unbelieving and hopeless. Turn to the Lord, ye prisoners of hope. Seek strength from God, the living God. Show an unwavering, humble faith in His power and His willingness to save. When in faith we take hold of His strength, He will change, wonderfully change, the most hopeless, discouraging outlook. He will do this for the glory of His name."[50]

"Hallowed Be Thy Name" is the fact that we are approaching God, the Creator of the universe, the mighty and majestic God. We must realize that when we pray, we are entering into the audience chamber of the most high God and that we should enter in with reverence, awe and respect! We cannot come before Him with any kind of attitude or with disrespect! We are coming before the Almighty God, the God who spoke and things were done!

The word "hallowed" means to be holy or honored. The psalmist writes in Psalm 111:9,

> "He sent redemption unto his people: he hath commanded his covenant for ever: holy and reverend *is* his name."

God's name stands for His character. "The name of God is holy, or hallowed, because God Himself is holy. We hallow His name by acknowledging His holiness of character and by permitting Him to reproduce that character in us."[51] "The angels veil their faces in His presence. The cherubim and the bright and holy seraphim approach His throne with solemn reverence. How much more should we, finite, sinful beings, come in a reverent manner before the Lord, our Maker."[52] "You cannot hallow His name, you cannot represent Him to the world, unless in life and character you represent the very life and character of God. This you can do only through the acceptance of the grace and righteousness of Christ."[53]

---

[50] Ellen White, *Prophet and Kings*, (Pacific Press Publishing, Nampa, ID, 1917), p. 260
[51] Ellen White, *SDA Commentary* Vol. 5, (Review & Harold Publishing, Hagerstown, MD, 1956), p. 346, 347
[52] Ellen White, *Thoughts From the Mount of Blessing*, (Pacific Press Publishing, Boise, Idaho), p. 106
[53] *Ibid*, p. 107

When we hallow His name, it is to say that we will never dishonor His name by the life we live. That we will never spoil His name by the way we act or carry ourselves. It means that our life will always reflect the character of God! Are the words that you use dishonoring God? Is what you watch on television or the internet dishonoring God? Is your life dishonoring the Lord? When we say "hallowed be thy name," what we are really saying is "for I do always those things that please him" John 8:29. We should never want to dishonor God in the light of God's love! One Christian theologian put it this way,

> "Nothing is clearer and unshakable to me than the purpose of the universe is for the hallowing of God's name. His kingdom comes for THAT. His will is done for THAT. Humans have bread-sustained life for THAT. Sins are forgiven for THAT. Temptation is escaped for THAT."[54]

What's the key to honoring His name? It is to recognize that He is gracious, caring, loving, all powerful and yielding to His Holy Spirit. To live a holy life before the world!

---

[54] Mark Finley, *Our Deepest Prayer: Hallowed Be Your Name*, 1-9-11.

1.) What was the difference between the way the disciples prayed and the way Jesus prayed?

_____

_____

2.) What does the first part of the prayer signify?

_____

_____

3.) There are at least two concepts in the Lord's Prayer. What are they?

_____

_____

4.) How does knowing that we have a heavenly Father impact our lives?

_____

_____

5.) We have a _____ _____ who cares for us _____. He's _____ to _____ our _____. He is _____ and _____.

6.) What does it mean to "hallow' God's name?

_____

_____

7.) How is it easy to dishonor God's name?

_____

_____

8.) What are the keys to honoring God's name?

_____

_____

CHAPTER 10

THE LORD'S PRAYER: PART 2

"After this manner therefore pray ye: Our Father which art in heaven, Hallowed be thy name. Thy kingdom come. Thy will be done in earth, as it is in heaven. Give us this day our daily bread. And forgive us our debts, as we forgive our debtors. And lead us not into temptation, but deliver us from evil: For thine is the kingdom, and the power, and the glory, for ever. Amen" Matthew 6:9-13.

"Thy kingdom come." When we pray "Thy kingdom come" what we are saying is for God to take our minds out of this world and focus it on the eternal world.

"My kingdom is not of this world: if my kingdom were of this world, then would my servants fight" John 18:36.

The kingdom within us is: the reign of Christ in our hearts as King of kings and Lord of lords. That there's nothing else but Jesus on the throne of our hearts. We can never acknowledge His coming kingdom with meaning unless His kingdom reigns first in our hearts. Matthew 25:34 declares,

"Then shall the King say unto them on his right hand, Come, ye blessed of my Father, inherit the kingdom prepared for you from the foundation of the world."

When we pray this prayer, it's the longing of the heart for God's kingdom. We're praying that the interest of God's kingdom be our interest. The building up of His kingdom is our supreme desire. We're asking God to come into hearts and transform us into His image.

When we pray this prayer, "Thy kingdom come" what we are saying is that we want peace to reign in our hearts. That we want His name to be honored among all nations.

We long for the day when all the forces of evil and wickedness are banished throughout the universe! We long for the day when Revelation 21:4 is fulfilled. When God will wipe away all tears and there shall be no more death, sorrow or sickness.

We pray "Thy kingdom come" that your kingdom come not mine. That your name be honored and not mine. As we pray, we'll understand that we have an obligation to share this message with others! That God's interests are our interests. That the up building of His kingdom is our supreme desire. The joys of His kingdom is our delight.

We are sick of a world where there is injustice, suffering, sadness, sickness, heartache and death. We are sick of a world where there's famine and death plaguing the people. When we pray "Thy kingdom come" is a prayer that is not only prayed with our lips, but with our lives! Are we living a kingdom life? Are our lives reflecting God's kingdom?

When we pray "Thy kingdom come" we're praying for the fulfillment of Revelation 11:15 that says,

> "And the seventh angel sounded; and there were great voices in heaven, saying, The kingdoms of this world are become *the kingdoms* of our Lord, and of his Christ; and he shall reign for ever and ever."

We are praying for God's kingdom to reign forever and ever! That's the kingdom that we are praying for and looking forward to. Jesus will reign forever and ever! A kingdom that will have no end! Daniel 7:27,

> "And the kingdom and dominion, and the greatness of the kingdom under the whole heaven, shall be given to the people of the saints of the most High, whose kingdom *is* an everlasting kingdom."

God's kingdom will be given to the saints forever and He will be their King forever and ever! Amen.

"Thy kingdom come."
"Thy will be done."

Within our prayers, we can appear to be very selfish, always wanting our desires and wants met. Prayer can become selfish at times. From the book, *Praying God's Heart*, the author writes,

> "One of the strangest things about prayer is that it can be the most selfish activity in the world. Prayer can be merely seeking to use God for one's own purposes.... But the problem comes when the focus in prayer is primarily on us and what we want. What we are really doing when we pray that way is trying to get God to be our servant. But He is not our servant. He is our Lord and Master and we are His servants."[55]

Our prayers should focus on God and that our lives are in harmony with His will. How do you know that you're praying God's will? How do you know that you're not seeking your own will when it comes to prayer? We will never know God's will unless we are willing to give up the

---

[55] Alvin VanderGriend, *Praying God's Heart*, (PrayerShop Publishing, Terre Haute, IN, 2010), p. 37

things we want most. We need to come before God seeking His ways and desires for our lives. Matthew 26:39,

> "O my Father, if it be possible, let this cup pass from me: nevertheless not as I will, but as thou *wilt*."

This portion of the prayer is surrendering our wills to God. He has to have complete control of our hearts. When this happens, He can mold and shape us. He "works in us to will and to do of His good pleasure" Phil. 2:13.

When we pray "Thy will be done" we are saying that we want our lives to be governed by the will of God. We come before God seeking His will. The psalmist declares in Psalm 40:8,

> "I delight to do thy will, O my God: yea, thy law *is* within my heart."

There comes a time in the Christian life, when you only want what God wants.

The prayer "Thy will be done" is a prayer where the reign of evil on this earth will be ended. That sin may ever be destroyed. And that the kingdom of righteousness will be forever established. Jesus wants to establish the principles of His eternal kingdom in us so that we might be able to live in the eternal kingdom of heaven!

Looking at the prayer, we observe three petitions: "Hallowed be Thy name, Thy kingdom come and Thy will be done." The first half of the prayer, Jesus teaches us that His name is to be hallowed, His kingdom to be established and His will to be performed. When we place His name above everything else, we can ask in confidence that our needs may be supplied. When honoring His name is our priority. When longing for His kingdom to be our greatest desire. When doing His will is the goal of our lives. Then we can claim His promise that the riches of heaven are ours by faith. He will meet each of our needs. He will never let us down.

"Give us this day our daily bread" is a request for today. There's no need to be concerned about tomorrow or the stresses that it might bring. God has promised to supply all our needs in Philippians 4:19. Just as God met the needs of the children of Israel in the wilderness, God will also meet our needs. He has not forgotten about our needs and desires. Ellen Whites writes,

> "When you have thus made God's service your first interest, you may ask with confidence that your own needs may be supplied. If you have renounced self and given yourself to Christ you are a member of the family of God, and everything in the Father's house is for you. All the treasures of God are opened to you, both the world that now is and that which is to come. The ministry of angels, the gift of His Spirit, the labors of His servants—all are for you. The world, with everything in it, is yours so far as it can do you good."[56]

---

[56] Ellen White, *Thoughts From the Mount of Blessing*, (Pacific Press Publishing, Boise, Idaho), p. 110

When we pray "give us this day our daily bread" we must trust in God to supply all our needs. If we don't trust Him now when things are plenty, then when the crisis comes, the prayer will be meaningless.

The Bible does predict in Revelation that a time will come when we cannot buy or sell. This is not an illusion, or something of our imagination. This is real and will come to pass. God says that our needs will be supplied! Isaiah 33:16 says that our bread and water shall be given to us, so we have nothing to fear. When we pray this prayer, we're saying God I trust You. God I believe that You will do it.

When we pray, "give us this day our daily bread" is not only for our physical food, but also for our spiritual need. John 6:51 Jesus says,

> "I am the living bread which came down from heaven."

We are not just praying for God to supply our everyday needs, but for Him to supply our spiritual needs. Our souls long after God so that we might be filled with His Holy Spirit.

This hunger of the soul is only satisfied when we seek His presence, kneel in His presence and read His Word. So when we pray "give us this day our daily bread" we are praying that He will instill in us trust that He'll supply our needs and that He Himself will come as the bread of life and feed us.

"Forgive us our debts as we forgive our debtors" has within it an important element that people overlook. We are forgiven as we forgive others! This is important! Matthew 6:14, 15,

> "For if ye forgive men their trespasses, your heavenly Father will also forgive you:
> But if ye forgive not men their trespasses, neither will your Father forgive your trespasses."

God in His loving mercy so freely forgives us of our sins. As a result of God's mercy, many want to be forgiven of their sins, yet they do not forgive others. When this happens, God will not forgive us of our sins! Regardless of the wrong done, Christians are to have the attitude of forgiveness toward others!

Forgiveness to us from God is motivated by God's love.

That love from God is supposed to touch our hearts and transform us, which in turn creates love within our hearts, which creates love for our brothers and sisters who have wronged us."[57] From the book *Testimonies to the Church*, Vol. 5, p. 170,

> "One of the most common sins, and one that is attended with most pernicious results, is the indulgence of an unforgiving spirit. How many will cherish animosity or revenge and then bow before God and ask to be forgiven as they forgive. Surely they can have no true sense of the import of this prayer or they would not dare to take it upon their lips."[58]

---

[57] Roy Rugless, *Teach Us To pray* (Used by Permissioon)
[58] Ellen White, *Testimonies for the Church, Vol. 5*, (Pacific Press Publishing, Boise, Idaho), p. 170

From the book *Christ Object Lessons*, she pens "Nothing can justify an unforgiving spirit. He who is unmerciful toward others shows that he himself is not a partaker of God's pardoning grace. In God's forgiveness the heart of the erring one is drawn close to the great heart of Infinite Love."[59]

She continues the thought and says "He who is unforgiving cuts off the very channel through which alone he can receive mercy from God. We should not think that unless those who have injured us confess the wrong we are justified in withholding from them our forgiveness."[60]

The apostle Paul writes in Ephesians 4:32,

> "And be ye kind one to another, tenderhearted, forgiving one another, even as God for Christ's sake hath forgiven you."

We forgive, because we are forgiven. Not because the other person is worthy of our forgiveness, but Christ has forgiven us. The failure to forgive others could cause our own souls to be lost and this is an important fact! Our being forgiven is directly in our ability to forgive others! Bitterness, resentment and a lack of forgiveness poisons our relationship with the Lord! Forgiving others releases the stress and anxiety that a person might experience. Forgiving is more for the person than the one being forgiven! It's a stress release! Once we have forgiven others, there won't be any condemnation by God, because of the act of forgiving others. Romans 8:1 says,

> "There *is* therefore now no condemnation to them which are in Christ Jesus."

And there will be peace in the soul, because of your forgiving others

---

[59] Ellen White, *Christ's Object Lessons*, (Pacific Press Publishing Association, Washington, D. C., 1941), p. 251
[60] Ellen White, *Thoughts From the Mount of Blessing*, (Pacific Press Publishing, Boise, Idaho), p. 113

1.) What are the longings of the heart when we pray?

_____

_____

2.) What is the building up of God's kingdom?

_____

_____

3.) What does it mean to pray "thy kingdom come'?

_____

_____

4.) Even though our prayers are to be heavenward, what is the problem within our prayers?

_____

_____

5.) What does it mean to pray "thy will be done"?

_____

_____

6.) What is the important element that people forget when praying the Lord's Prayer?

_____

_____

7.) What is the motivation for God forgiving us?

_____

_____

8.) What happens to an unforgiving person?

_____

_____

THE LORD'S PRAYER: PART 3

"After this manner therefore pray ye: Our Father which art in heaven, Hallowed be thy name. Thy kingdom come. Thy will be done in earth, as it is in heaven. Give us this day our daily bread. And forgive us our debts, as we forgive our debtors. And lead us not into temptation, but deliver us from evil: For thine is the kingdom, and the power, and the glory, for ever. Amen" Matthew 6:9-13.

"Lead us not into temptation"

"Let no man say when he is tempted, I am tempted of God: for God cannot be tempted with evil, neither tempteth he any man" James 1:13.

God, our Father, who provides for our every need will never lead us into temptation. This goes against His will for our lives! Temptation used in the New Testament can also mean "test or prove" men, but He never tempts them to sin. James asserts in James 1:13,

"Let no man say when he is tempted, I am tempted of God: for God cannot be tempted with evil, neither tempteth he any man."

God longs to develop our characters so that we might be more like Him. "God in His great love is seeking to develop in us the precious graces of His Spirit. He permits us to encounter obstacles, persecution, and hardships, not as a curse, but as the greatest blessing of our lives. Every temptation resisted, every trial bravely borne, gives us a new experience and advances us in the work of character building."[61]

When we pray "lead me not into temptation," what we're saying is that God will not allow us to be tempted or tested above that which we are able. That He promises to help us make it through those dark and trying times! It's a promise that we can claim.

The devil seeks to draw us away from God by leading us into temptation. Our nature is weak and fallen, most of the time, we will fall. That's why when we pray this portion of the prayer, we

---

[61] *Ibid*, p. 117

need to ask God to help us resist the devil. We need to allow God to lead and guide instead of us trying to guide ourselves. The psalmist says in Psalm 32:8,

> "I will instruct thee and teach thee in the way which thou shalt go: I will guide thee with mine eye."

"When the soul surrenders itself to Christ, a new power takes possession of the new heart. A change is wrought which man can never accomplish for himself. It is a supernatural work, bringing a supernatural element into human nature."[62] This is imperative because if not, we will come under the control of Satan.

"The only safeguard against evil is the indwelling of Christ in the heart through faith in His righteousness. It is because selfishness exists in our hearts that temptation has power over us. But when we behold the great love of God, selfishness appears to us in its hideous and repulsive character, and we desire to have it expelled from the soul. As the Holy Spirit glorifies Christ, our hearts are softened and subdued, the temptation loses its power, and the grace of Christ transforms the character."[63]

Not only that, He has the power to deal with anything that needs to be dealt with. It is with that thought that we end this prayer – with confidence – with faith knowing that God is going to work it out because He cares about us and He is able. We give Him honor, glory, praise and thanks for what He is going to do and has already done!

[62] Ellen White, *Desire of Ages*, (Pacific Press Publishing Association, Nampa, ID, 2002), p. 324
[63] Ellen White, *Thoughts From the Mount of Blessing*, (Pacific Press Publishing, Boise, Idaho), p. 118

1.) When using the word for tempted, could there be another word used? If so, what is it?

_____

_____

2.) He _____ us to encounter _____, _____, and _____, not as

a _____, but as the _____ blessing of _____ _____.

3.) When we are praying this portion of the prayer, what are we to do?

_____

_____

4.) What is the only safe guard we have against evil?

_____

_____

5.) But when we _____ the great _____ of _____, _____ appears to us in its

_____ and _____ _____, and we _____ to have it

_____ from the _____.

6.) How do we end this prayer?

_____

_____

CHAPTER 12

INTERCESSORY PRAYER

"Wherefore he is able also to save them to the uttermost that come unto God by him, seeing he ever liveth to make intercession for them" Hebrews 7:25.

"Cease not to give thanks for you, making mention of you in my prayers" Ephesians 1:16.

Intercessory prayer is a biblical concept that many of the Bible writers used in their prayer life. Many of the Bible writers prayed for themselves, but also had prayers of intercession. It's praying that God's will be done upon earth and that the stronghold of the enemy will be broken.

However, when we intercede for others, we unite with Jesus in His mighty work of intercession. The writer of Hebrews asserts, "He ever liveth to make intercession" Hebrews 7:25. Webster's New World College Dictionary defines intercession as "the act of interceding; mediation, pleading, or prayer in behalf of another or others." The primary focus of the prayer is on the salvation of others! It's not focused on your wants, desires or ambitions, but that God will reach and touch the hearts of the ones you're praying for.

When we intercede for someone, we want God's will to be done in their lives. We want God to save them from judgment or His wrath. The prophet Ezekiel says in Ezekiel 33:11,

> "As I live, saith the Lord GOD, I have no pleasure in the death of the wicked; but
> that the wicked turn from his way and live: turn ye, turn ye from your evil ways;
> for why will ye die, O house of Israel?"

Cheryl Sacks makes the difference between prayer and intercessory prayer. She writes, "All intercession is prayer, but not all prayer is intercession. Prayer is talking with God. Intercession is petitioning God for the needs of another."[64]

Intercession creates a meeting between God and the person you're praying for. The Hebrew word for intercession is "pagha" which means "to meet", "to push against", "to attack", "to urge a request", "to make peace", to "dissolve a relationship."[65] When we intercede for the lost, we ask God to dissolve the relationship between Satan and the person we are praying for. We can see

---

[64] Cheryl Sacks, *The Prayer Saturated Church*, (NavPress, Colorado Springs, CO 80935, 2004), p. 160

[65] Dennis Smith, *Spirit Baptism and Prayer*, (Tyndale House Publishers, Inc., 2008), p. 52

this in Luke 22:31-32, when Christ says to Peter, "Simon, Simon, behold, Satan hath desired to have you, that he may sift you as wheat; but I have prayed for you." Christ prayed that Peter's faith will not fail him. John 17, where Christ's prayed for the disciples and for believers that they be "one" as He and the Father are one.

Jesus' life was one of prayer. He prayed in the early morning hours. He prayed for strength to start His day. He prayed for others and His disciples. "Every one of His prayers was faith-filled, heartfelt and fervent."[66] Jesus loved communing with His Father. It gave Him strength for the day. Everything that He did was to glorify His Father.

Jesus was the ultimate intercessor. In the majority of His prayers, Christ interceded for others and He cared for their well-being and wanted to see them saved in His kingdom. His last prayer recorded in John 17, is one of intercession. He interceded for Himself, (verses 1-5), He interceded for His disciples, their protection, their joy, their sanctification and their place with Him in glory, (verses 6-19), and Jesus interceded for all believers that they might be one as He is with the Father, (verses 20-26). "The thrust of this prayer is Christ's ardent desire for His disciples and all believers to share what He enjoys with the Father; the unity, mutual love and trust, faithfulness, truth, unity, joy, consecration and mission."[67]

The Lord's Prayer is a prayer of intercession, because it's broken into several parts. First, it focuses on God's heart: His glory, His kingdom and His will. The next section deals with our lives: His provision, His pardon and His protection from the evil one."[68] "When we seek God in earnest intercession for others, He promises to make us a channel of His life-giving power. The river of water of life from God's throne is poured out through us to touch other hearts. Our prayers and our faith make a dramatic difference in their lives."[69]

Mark Finley gives four reasons why we should intercede for others: 1) "Prayer enables God to speak to us about the sins in our own lives that are a hindrance to successful soul-winning. 2.) Prayer deepens our desire concerning the thing for which we are praying. 3.) Prayer puts us in touch with divine wisdom. 4.) Prayer enables God to work more powerfully than He could if we did not pray."[70]

Intercessory prayer is giving God the opportunity to step into the lives of people that we want to see saved in God's kingdom! There's nothing more important than to pray for those who are in darkness! The apostle Paul reminds us that God is not "willing that any should perish, but that all should come to repentance." To destroy is a strange work for Him. He's interceding that all will be saved!

---

[66] Alvin VanderGriend, *Praying God's Heart*, (PrayerShop Publishing, Terre Haute, IN, 2010), p. 25
[67] Philip Samaan, *Christ's Way To Pray*, (Review and Herald Publishing Association, Hagerstown, MD, 2006), p.45
[68] Alvin VanderGriend, *Praying God's Heart*, (PrayerShop Publishing, Terre Haute, IN, 2010), p. 26
[69] Mark Finley, *Light Your World For God*, (Hart Books Publishers, 2002), p. 30
[70] *Ibid.,* p. 31-33

1.) How would you define intercessory prayer?

_____

_____

2.) What is the primary focus of intercessory prayer?

_____

_____

3.) What does the Hebrew word "pagha" means and how would you apply it to intercessory prayer?

_____

_____

4.) What is God's promise to us in the Lord's Prayer when we intercede for others?

_____

_____

5.) _____ was the ultimate _____. In the _____ of His _____,

_____ _____ for _____ and He _____ for their

_____-_____ and wanted to see them _____ in His_____.

6.) Mark Finley list 4 reasons why we need to intercede for others. List at least three of them.

_____

_____

INTERCESSORY PRAYER – CONT.

"Wherefore he is able also to save them to the uttermost that come unto God by him, seeing he ever liveth to make intercession for them" Hebrews 7:25.

"I exhort therefore, that, first of all, supplications, prayers, intercessions, and giving of thanks, be made for all men" 1 Timothy 2:1.

"And pray in the Spirit on all occasions with all kinds of prayers and requests. With this in mind, be alert and always keep on praying for all the saints" Ephesians 6:18, NIV.

As we stated at the beginning, intercession is praying for others and their salvation. It's allowing God to do things that He would not do otherwise. "The reality is that intercession is the ministry that God has given each of us.

And intercession allows Him to bless the world in ways that He could not if we did not pray. Our prayers can change the lives of others and change the world."[71] "However, it is essential that the believer pray for them so that God's power can be released in their life and Satan's power over them broken."[72]

We begin to lift up others in prayer so that the Holy Spirit can permeate their hearts and change their minds toward God. "God needs our prayers to aid in His work, not because He is not powerful enough without us, but because He has voluntarily limited Himself to allow humanity to participate in the salvation of the world."[73] The birthplace of intercessory prayer is in the heart of God! Just think, if church members were to intercede for the world, what a change there would be. Souls would be won to the kingdom of God and this would hasten His soon coming! From the book Christ's Object Lesson, the author writes,

> "As we seek to win others to Christ, bearing the burden of souls in our prayers,
> our own hearts will throb with the quickening influence of God's grace; our own

---

[71] Carrol J. Shewmaker, *When We Pray For Others*, (Review & Harold Publishing, Hagerstown, MD, 1995), p. 21

[72] Dennis Smith, *Spirit Baptism and Prayer*, (Tyndale House Publishers, Inc., 2008), p. 54

[73] Carrol J. Shewmaker, *When We Pray For Others*, (Review & Harold Publishing, Hagerstown, MD, 1995), p. 20

affections will glow with more divine fervor; our whole Christian life will be more of a reality, more earnest, more prayerful."[74]

The grace of God will flow to us, through us and for us as we intercede for others. It will give us power to fight the devil with the power of prayer! We have said it so often, "prayer changes things." However, we must understand that "prayer is not only a necessity for the salvation of others. It also plays a vital role in our own salvation. Prayer or the lack of it for others reveals much about where our heart is. If we have the heart of Jesus we will have a loving concern for others and will be eager to pray for them."[75]

We cannot forget that the great controversy is still waging over the hearts and minds of people! The enemy wants nothing more than to deceive, destroy and kill as many people as he can. In order for us to be victorious, we must put on the whole armor of God. Ephesians 6:12 tells us, "For we wrestle not against flesh and blood, but against principalities, against powers, against the rulers of the darkness of this world, against spiritual wickedness in high places."

The apostle believed in prayer and intercessory prayer. "He did not believe prayer to be some kind of psychotherapy that would make him feel better. He believed that, through prayer, he could touch the heart of God. He was convinced God would work miracles through prayer."[76]

The Bible points out the significance of intercessory prayer. Moses interceded for the children of Israel when they made a golden calf. God was going to blot them out of existence and make a great nation with Moses. Read about it in Exodus 32. From the book *Patriarchs and Prophets*, p. 319,

> "As Moses interceded for Israel, his timidity was lost in his deep interest and love for those for whom he had, in the hands of God, been the means of doing so much. The Lord listened to his pleadings, and granted his unselfish prayer. God had proved His servant; He had tested his faithfulness and his love for that erring, ungrateful people, and nobly had Moses endured the trial. His interest in Israel sprang from no selfish motive. The prosperity of God's chosen people was dearer to him than personal honor, dearer than the privilege of becoming the father of a mighty nation. God was pleased with his faithfulness, his simplicity of heart, and his integrity, and He committed to him, as a faithful shepherd, the great charge of leading Israel to the Promised Land."[77]

In his intercession for the people, he pleads for three things with God. First, he pleads the Lord's integrity. Israel was still His people and he had done so much for them. He would not give up on them now. God's name was at stake. Second, he pleads the Lord's honor. If God destroyed them, what would the surrounding nations think of Him? They would rejoice and their accusations would prove true, that instead of bringing them into the wilderness to serve God, He brought them there to destroy them. Third, he pleads the Lord's word or promises. God

[74] Ellen White, *Christ's Object Lessons*, (Pacific Press Publishing Association, Washington, D. C., 1941), p. 354

[75] Dennis Smith, *Spirit Baptism and Prayer*, (Tyndale House Publishers, Inc., 2008), p. 60

[76] Mark Finley, *Prayer Makes a Difference*, (Hart Research Publishers, Fallbrook, CA., 2003), p. 5

[77] Ellen White, *Patriarchs and Prophets*, (Pacific Press Publishers, Nampa, ID, 2005), p. 319

had promised Abraham, Isaac and Jacob that He would give them the land of promise, flowing with milk and honey. God's word was now at stake. Would He renege on what He said? Moses' intercession for the people, encouraged God to turn from His wrath and spare the people.

In Ezekiel 22:30, Israel had departed from following the commands of God and started serving others gods. Their wickedness had reached up to heaven and God was going to pronounce judgment on them. God sought a man to stand in the gap, but found none. No one was found to intercede for the people and their sins! Since God could not find someone to intercede for the people, His indignation was poured out upon the people! The Bible says in Ezekiel 22:31, "Therefore, have I poured out mine indignation upon them; I have consumed them with the fire of my wrath." This text lets us know the importance of intercessory prayer! It's a prayer that is God inspired. God looks for individuals praying for others! "The Lord will hear our prayers for the conversion of souls."[78]

"Intercessory prayer is cooperation with God. He chooses to have us cooperate with Him in order to bring His plans for the world to complete fruition. God could bypass us humans if He chose to do so. He is sovereign, almighty and all wise. He doesn't need our permission to act. But He has chosen us in on the process and has prepared us to be intercessors through the work of His Son and His Holy Spirit."[79]

Abraham interceded for Sodom. He pleaded with the Lord about finding some righteous people. If he found people that were righteous, would He spare the city? He begins asking God to spare the city if 50 people could be found in it. He starts with fifty (50) and goes all the way down to ten (10). Abraham was concerned about the salvation of those people living within the city! We should have that same desire to see people saved in God's kingdom! God said that if ten (10) righteous people could be found, He would spare them. Ellen White writes,

> "Love for perishing souls inspired Abraham's prayer. While he loathed the sins of that corrupt city, he desired that the sinners might be saved. His deep interest for Sodom shows the anxiety that we should feel for the impenitent. We should cherish hatred of sin, but pity and love for the sinner. All around us are souls going down to ruin as hopeless, as terrible, as that which befell Sodom."[80]

Our prayers must not be focused on self and what we want and desire! Our prayers should first and foremost be centered upon God and what He has done for us! Then focus upon the salvation of others! We should want to behold individuals saved in God's kingdom! That's why the Bible admonishes us to pray for one another! 1 Timothy 2:1-3 says,

> "The first thing I want you to do is pray. Pray every way you know how, for everyone you know. Pray especially for rulers and their governments to rule well so we can be quietly about our business of living simply, in humble contemplation. This is the way our Savior God wants us to live" The Message Bible.

---

[78] Ellen White, *Messages to Young People*, (Review and Herald Publishing Association, Hagerstown, MD, 1930), p. 315

[79] Alvin VanderGriend, *Praying God's Heart*, (PrayerShop Publishing, Terre Haute, IN, 2010), p. 50, 51

[80] Ellen White, *Patriarchs and Prophets*, (Pacific Press Publishers, Nampa, ID, 2005), p. 140

1.) What is the ministry that God gave us?

_____

_____

2.) Where is the birthplace of intercessory prayer?

_____

_____

3.) How can we defeat the powers of the enemy?

_____

_____

4.) When Moses interceded for the children of Israel, he pleaded for three things. What are they?

_____

_____

5.) True or false. Intercession is God inspired.

_____

_____

6.) _____ or the _____ of it for _____ _____ much about

_____ our _____ _____.

CHAPTER 14

HINDRANCES TO PRAYER

"If I regard iniquity in my heart, the Lord will not hear me:" Psalm 66:18

"But your iniquities have separated between you and your God, and your sins have hid his face from you, that he will not hear" Isaiah 59:2.

More than anything else, we would love to have our prayers answered, especially if it is urgent or an emergency. We want God to hear our prayers and answer them as fast as possible. No delay or time waited or anything else that would impede the answer to the prayer. However, there are some things that will hinder us from receiving an answer to our prayers. When we receive an answer to our prayers, it is based upon our connection to Christ!

The Bible makes it clear that known sins in the life can hinder the answer to our prayer. The above texts make that clear. Sin can separate us from God. It makes our prayers powerless! Not only does it separate, but sin makes us want to be isolated from religious things and people. John Maxwell stresses that,

> "Sin demands to have a man by himself. It withdraws him from the community. The more isolated a person is, the more destructive will be the power of sin over him and the more disastrous is this isolation. Sin wants to remain unknown. It shuns the light. In the darkness of the unexpressed it poisons the whole being of a person."[81]

Another hindrance to answer prayer is doubt or unbelief. In the story recorded in Mark 9:14, a father brings his son to the disciples to be cured from demon possession. The disciples failed to cast out the demon from the boy. From the book *Desire of Ages*, the author writes,

> "The multitude looked on with bated breath, the father in an agony of hope and fear. Jesus asked, 'How long is it ago since this came unto him?'

---

[81] John Maxwell, *Partners in Prayer*, (Nelson Books Publishers, Nashville, TN, 1996), p. 53

"The father told the story of long years of suffering, and then, as if he could endure no more, exclaimed, 'If Thou canst do anything, have compassion on us, and help us.' 'If Thou canst!' Even now the father questioned the power of Christ."[82]

The reason why the disciples did not cast out the demon was because of their unbelief. Ellen White writes,

"The nine disciples were yet pondering upon the bitter fact of their own failure; and when Jesus was once more alone with them, they questioned, "Why could not we cast him out?" Jesus answered them. "Because of your unbelief: for verily I say unto you, If ye have faith as a grain of mustard seed, ye shall say unto this mountain, Remove hence to yonder place; and it shall remove; and nothing shall be impossible unto you. Howbeit this kind goeth not out but by prayer and fasting."

"Their unbelief, that shut them out from deeper sympathy with Christ, and the carelessness with which they regarded the sacred work committed to them, had caused their failure in the conflict with the powers of darkness. Instead of strengthening their faith by prayer and meditation on the words of Christ, they had been dwelling on their discouragements and personal grievances."[83]

Hebrews 11:6 states that it is impossible to please God without faith. "Without faith it is impossible to intercede powerfully and effectively. Prayer is not just throwing wishes toward heaven with the hope that something will happen. It is trusting that God will act in accord with His nature and His promises."[84]

Disobedience is another hindrance to having our prayers answered. Our relationship with God will keep us in line with His will and commands. In order to have answers to our prayers, we must obey all that He requires! "Obedience should be a natural outgrowth of faith in God. He that obeys God, trusts Him; he that trust Him, obeys Him."[85]

It's about having that trusting relationship with God. Knowing that God hear our prayers. 1 John 3:21, 22 says,

"Beloved, if our heart condemn us not, *then* have we confidence toward God. And whatsoever we ask, we receive of him, because we keep his commandments, and do those things that are pleasing in his sight."

Still another hindrance to prayer is selfishness. The parable in Luke 11:1-13 shows the act of giving. We must have the same spirit of giving as Christ possessed. Ellen White asserts,

---

[82] Ellen White, *Desires of Ages*, (Pacific Press Publishing Association, Nampa, ID, 2002), p. 428

[83] *Ibid.*, p. 430-431

[84] Alvin VanderGriend, *Praying God's Heart*, (PrayerShop Publishing, Terre Haute, IN, 2010), p. 161

[85] John Maxwell, *Partners in Prayer*, (Nelson Books Publishers, Nashville, TN, 1996), p. 55

"Our prayers are not to be a selfish asking, merely for our own benefit. We are to ask that we may give. The principle of Christ's life must be the principle of our lives."[86]

She continues and says,

"Our mission to the world is not to serve or please ourselves; we are to glorify God by co-operating with Him to save sinners. We are to ask blessings from God that we may communicate to others. The capacity for receiving is preserved only by imparting. We cannot continue to receive heavenly treasure without communicating to those around us."[87]

Indifference to human need is another hindrance to prayer. God has a heart that loves to give. He loved us so much that He gave His only Son to die for the sins of the world. Believers in turn also ought to do the same to those in need. Proverbs 21:13,

"Whoso stoppeth his ears at the cry of the poor, he also shall cry himself, but shall not be heard."

"God links His willingness to hear our prayers to our willingness to hear the cries of the poor. If we are praying for God to meet the needs of the poor but are not willing to step up to meet those needs, when and where this is possible, we should not expect God to answer. Prayers must also be matched with actions. God expects intercessors to be thoughtful and lovingly involved in the lives of those with needs. If our ears are open to the cries of the poor, the cries that come from 'the least the last and the lost,' then God's ears will be open to our prayers."[88]

---

[86] Ellen White, *Christ's Object Lessons*, (Pacific Press Publishing Association, Washington, D. C., 1941), p. 142
[87] *Ibid.*, p. 142, 143
[88] Alvin VanderGriend, *Praying God's Heart*, (PrayerShop Publishing, Terre Haute, IN, 2010), p. 160

1.) We know that sin separates us from God; but what else does it do?

_____

_____

2.) Why was it difficult for the disciples to cast out the demon from the man's son?

_____

_____

3.) Our _____ with _____ will _____ us _____ _____ with His

_____ and _____.

4.) What is our mission to the world when it comes to God in prayer?

_____

_____

5.) Name at least three hindrance in prayer.

_____

_____

6.) God links what to what when it comes to prayer?

_____

_____

CHAPTER 15

THE POWER OF PRAISE

"Oh that men would praise the LORD for his goodness, and for his wonderful works to the children of men! For he satisfieth the longing soul, and filleth the hungry soul with goodness" Psalm 107:8, 9

The book of Psalms are filled with praises to God and His goodness. The text above expresses the fact the men ought to praise God for His goodness and wonderful works towards men. We should praise God for who He is. The angels cry out daily "holy, holy, holy" to God daily. The angels praise Him because He is God!

Praise should come forth out of our mouths every day. We should praise God for what He has done for us! Praise should flow from us because God has been so good to us and has shown us all His benefits! "We should praise God for the blessed hope held out before us in the great plan of redemption, we should praise Him for the heavenly inheritance and for His rich promises; praise Him that Jesus lives to intercede for us."[89] David asserts,

> "I will extol thee, my God, O king; and I will bless thy name for ever and ever. Every day will I bless thee; and I will praise thy name for ever and ever. Great *is* the LORD, and greatly to be praised; and his greatness *is* unsearchable" Psalm 145:1-3.

We are placing God above everything and everybody. We're praising Him for His mighty acts. It changes our attitude towards Him and others. When we're praising God, our focus is upon God and all that He has done! Depression, anger, frustration and anxiety disappears. Our failures and disappointments turns into successes because of Christ's strength!

When we praise God, any suggestions that Satan tries to do is quickly erased, because our minds are on Christ and His goodness! We see from heavens perspective and not from our perspective. Giving praise to God is focusing upon His goodness and His grace. The focus is no longer on ourselves!

Even if our prayers of praise to God sounds inadequate and weak, the Holy Spirit takes it to God and presents it the way that it should be. When we learn to praise God first in our prayers, we'll join in the chorus of the angels in lifting up the Lord! We'll praise God for all that He has done and if He does nothing else for us, we'll still praise Him! "To praise God in fullness and

---

[89] Ellen White, *Patriarchs and Prophets*, (Pacific Press Publishers, Nampa, ID, 2005), p. 289

sincerity of heart is as much a duty as is prayer. We are to show to the world and to all the heavenly intelligences that we appreciate the wonderful love of God for fallen humanity and that we are expecting larger and yet larger blessings from His infinite fullness."[90]

"Even before we thank God for what He has done for us, we should praise Him just for who He is. God is worthy of praise whether He ever blesses us or not! From age to age, He is the most high God, ever holy, ever true, King of kings and Lord of lords, full of everlasting loving-kindness and tender mercy. His praises never cease and regardless of what happens to us, our whole purpose in life is to swell the chorus."[91]

During our most difficult situation, we need to praise God! It gives us victory over the enemy. It gives us assurance that God will hear and answer our prayer! Daniel prayed when his life was threatened in Daniel 6:10. While in prison, Paul and Silas prayed and sang praises while being held in chains. "If we do not praise God, we will not see God work in our behalf as He would like. By the way, praise to God is not for His benefit. It is for our benefit. It lifts our sights upward to God and increases our faith in Him and His delivering power."[92]

Testimony to the Church, vol. 5, page 317,

> "We do not pray any too much, but we are too sparing of giving thanks. If the loving-kindness of God called forth more thanksgiving and praise, we would have far more power in prayer. We would abound more and more in the love of God and have more bestowed to praise Him for. You who complain that God does not hear your prayers, change your present order and mingle praise with your petitions. When you consider His goodness and mercies you will find that He will consider your wants."[93]

When we are praising God, it transforms our daily life, as well as transforming our prayers! Nothing can be substituted for praise! Praising God brings honor to Him and brings to the heavenly host. Praising God place fear and terror in the hearts of the devil! Praise clears the atmosphere of anything that is negative and that seems to be destructive! Praising God will increase your faith and give you the power to overcome any temptation! Praising God is something that we need to do more of! David declares in Psalm 150,

> "Praise ye the LORD. Praise God in his sanctuary: praise him in the firmament of his power. Praise him for his mighty acts: praise him according to his excellent greatness. Praise him with the sound of the trumpet: praise him with the psaltery and harp. Praise him with the timbrel and dance: praise him with stringed instruments and organs. Praise him upon the loud cymbals: praise him upon the high sounding cymbals. Let every thing that hath breath praise the LORD. Praise ye the LORD."

[90] Ellen White, *Christ's Object Lessons*, (Pacific Press Publishing Association, Washington, D. C., 1941), p. 299
[91] Tim Crosby, *A Passion for Prayer*, (Review and Herald Publishing, Hagerstown, MD, 1998), p. 31
[92] Dennis Smith, *Spirit Baptism and Prayer*, (Tyndale House Publishers, Inc., 2008), p.64
[93] Ellen White, *Testimonies For the Church*, Vol. 5, (Pacific Press Publishers, Boise, ID, 1948), p. 317

1.) When should we praise God?

_____

_____

2.) The Holy Spirit was given so that He could accomplish the work that God wanted Him to do through us. However, instead of relying upon Him, what has the church relied upon?

_____

_____

3.) When we praise God, several things occur. What are those things that occur?

_____

_____

4.) How important is the Holy Spirit in our lives?

_____

_____

5.) After we have learned to praise God, what happens?

_____

_____

6.) We are to _____ to the _____ and to all the _____ _____ that we _____ the _____ _____ of _____ for _____ _____ and that we are _____ larger and yet _____ *blessings* from His _____ fullness.

7.) What would happen if we learned to praise God more?

_____

_____

CHAPTER 16

FASTING AND PRAYER

"And he said unto them, 'This kind can come forth by nothing, but by prayer and fasting'" Mark 9:29.

"That ye may give yourselves to fasting and prayer;" 1 Corinthians 7."

When you read the Bible, you discover that many of God's people fasted and prayed in their lives. Fasting was a part of their spiritual life and if they wanted an answer to their prayers, they knew too fast and pray! We see people like Moses, David, Nehemiah, Daniel, Anna, Paul and even Jesus fasting. When there was something of importance and needed an answer, these individuals would fast and pray to find out God's will for their lives.

However, fasting has become almost obsolete in the Christian world today. Christians did not feel the need to fast and pray. Somehow fasting has lost its meaning and that people really don't need the power of God in their lives! Since it's not been taught or preached about, people think that it has been done away with. There is nowhere in the Bible where fasting has been eliminated! It is just as important as prayer!

Fasting is nothing more than doing without things that we like, such as food, drink or the pleasures we love. It's about seeking God's will for our lives! It is about staying connected with Him when we fast! The fast might be for a day, three days or even a week. The purpose of fasting is to abstain from things that you find pleasure in. It's focusing your heart and mind upon Christ. He becomes the center of your attention! Nothing else matters but placing Christ first in your thoughts!

However, we must remember that fasting is a spiritual endeavor! It's seeking God for answers to prayer. Fasting is something that is done ***intentional!*** Just because a person did not take the time to eat doesn't make it a fast!

"A fast is a conscious, intentional decision to abstain for a time from the pleasure of eating in order to gain vital spiritual benefits."[94]

Is there a command to fast in the Bible? Christ says in Matthew 6:16, "Moreover when ye fast" meaning that it is part of our Christian duty! He did not say "if you fast or maybe when

---

[94] Dr. Myles Munroe, *"Understanding the Purpose and Power of Prayer"* (New Kensington, PA: Whitaker House, 2002), p. 252

you do fast," but "when you fast." Prayer and fasting go hand and hand. One is just as important as the other! As stated earlier, fasting is to afflict the soul and that we might have the character and likeness of Jesus. "The object of the fast which God calls upon us to keep is not to afflict the body for the sin of the soul, but to aid us in perceiving the grievous character of sin, in humbling the heart before God and receiving His pardoning grace."[95]

In Matthew, Jesus shows the importance of prayer and fasting. When the father brought his devil possessed son to the disciples and ask them to rid him of the demons, these men tried but failed. They could not understand why they could not rid the boy of the demons. The Bible says in Matthew 17:18,

> "And Jesus rebuked the devil; and he departed out of him: and the child was cured from that very hour. Then came the disciples to Jesus apart, and said, 'Why could not we cast him out?' And Jesus said unto them, 'Because of your unbelief: for verily I say unto you, If ye have faith as a grain of mustard seed, ye shall say unto this mountain, Remove hence to yonder place; and it shall remove; and nothing shall be impossible unto you. Howbeit this kind goeth not out but by prayer and fasting.'"

The disciples did not place much thought into fasting and praying! They automatically thought that they could rid the boy of the demons! In order to have power with God, we need to fast and pray! We must believe that God is going to do what He said He would do! Ellen White from her book *Desire of Ages*, writes,

> "Instead of strengthening their faith by prayer and meditation on the words of Christ, they had been dwelling on their discouragements and personal grievances. In this state of darkness they had undertaken the conflict with Satan.
>
> "In order to succeed in such a conflict they must come to the work in a different spirit. Their faith must be strengthened by fervent prayer and fasting, and humiliation of heart.
>
> "They must be emptied of self, and be filled with the Spirit and power of God. Earnest, persevering supplication to God in faith—faith that leads to entire dependence upon God, and unreserved consecration to His work—can alone avail to bring men the Holy Spirit's aid in the battle against principalities and powers, the rulers of the darkness of this world, and wicked spirits in high places."[96]

It is important for us to keep our minds and hearts fixed upon Jesus and allow nothing to separate us from His love! We must have the faith that can move mountains! "Jesus made it very clear that prayer and fasting are essential factor in strong faith. Hence, if we want stronger faith

---

[95] Ellen White, *Thoughts From the Mount of Blessing*, (Pacific Press Publishing, Boise, Idaho), p. 87
[96] Ellen White, *Desire of Ages*, (Pacific Press Publishing Association, Nampa, ID, 2002), p. 431

to overcome Satan's influences in our lives and ministry for the Lord, fasting and praying must become a regular part of our Christian lives."[97]

There are some benefits when we fast. "Fasting enables us to increase our spiritual capacity. It exerts discipline over our physical appetites. Fasting does not change God; it changes us, and it transforms our prayers. Fasting allows us to receive guidance, wisdom, instruction and knowledge from God. Fasting enables us to receive the fullness of God's power for ministry. Fasting will develop a hunger for God as well as an intimacy with Him. Fasting often brings breakthroughs in difficult circumstances or in the lives of those who are resistant to the gospel."[98] The point is that fasting and prayer is no doubt a part of our Christian life! If we allow the Holy Spirit to dwell in us, we love to fast and prayer for spiritual power!

Are there concerns about your spiritual life? Do you seek a closer walk with the Lord? Do you want to know the will of God for your life? Is there a decision that has to be made? Fasting will answer all if not most of these questions. Fasting places us in the presence of God to know His will for our lives!

---

[97] Dennis Smith, *Spirit Baptism and Prayer*, (Tyndale House Publishers, Inc., 2008), p. 88

[98] Dr. Myles Munroe, *"Understanding the Purpose and Power of Prayer"* (New Kensington, PA: Whitaker House, 2002), p. 254-257

1.) Why do you think fasting has become almost obsolete in our society today?

_____

_____

2.) What is the purpose of fasting?

_____

_____

3.) Why is fasting intentional? Is there any confusion here when fasting?

_____

_____

4.) In Matthew 17, when the father brings his son to the disciples, explain why they failed and why that's important to us.

_____

_____

5.) A _____ is a _____, _____ decision to _____ for a _____ from the _____ of _____ in order to _____ vital spiritual _____.

6.) List at least three benefits of fasting.

_____

_____

CHAPTER 17

CONCLUSION

As we have concluded this workbook, I pray that prayer has become a major part of your life. As Christians, we cannot do without prayer in our lives! We must take the time out and pray for strength, power and to overcome sin. We must follow the example that Jesus left us in His prayer in Matthew 6.

When we stay connected to the source of power, the world will behold the image of Jesus in each of us! If ever there was a time to pray, it is now. The world that we live in, is in complete disarray! Our world needs prayer so that God's will can be done and that souls might be won to the kingdom of God!

Prayer is an invitation that God gives each of us to come into His presence and lay our cares at His feet. We have been admonished to come boldly before the throne of grace. How can we refuse such an invitation? If we refuse this invitation, we lose the connection that God wants us to have with Him!

Prayer is giving God permission to employ His power on the earth. If we did not pray, how could God's will be done on earth? Our prayers are needed for Him to intervene in the lives of those in whom we want to see saved!

We must understand that prayer is vital to our spiritual growth! It is just as important as breathing is to our existence! If we refuse or stop breathing, life would cease to exist. It is the same way with prayer. If we refuse or stop, our spiritual life will cease to exist! It is just that simple!

Prayer is something that's personal and intentional. In order to get something out of it, we must put something in it. What? Ourselves! When we come before God in prayer, we surrender our all to Him so that He can fill us with His Spirit! So that we can learn His will for our lives.

The more we understand the necessity of prayer, the more we would want to do it. Because it will enhance our relationship with God. Prayer plays a vital role in our salvation! We cannot overlook that prayer breaks the stronghold of the enemy!

"Satan is more afraid of the praying Christian than the active, working Christian, which is why he will do all in his power to keep you from becoming a Spirit-filled, Spirit-directed prayer intercessor for God."[99]

God had given us a divine invitation to pray and come to Him just as we are. He has promised

---

[99] Dennis Smith, *Spirit Baptism and Prayer*, (Tyndale House Publishers, Inc., 2008), p. 12

to take our cares and perplexities upon Himself. He says to us "Come and rest." Matthew 11:28-30 declares,

> "Come unto me, all *ye* that labour and are heavy laden, and I will give you rest. Take my yoke upon you, and learn of me; for I am meek and lowly in heart: and ye shall find rest unto your souls. For my yoke *is* easy, and my burden is light."

PRAYER IS A DIVINE INVITATION TO COME TO JESUS!

BIBLIOGRAPHY

Collins, Steven. *Christian Discipleship*, Hensley Publishing, Tulsa, OK, 1998.

Charles, H. B. JR., *It Happens After Prayer*, Moody publishers, Chicago, IL, 2013.

Crosby, Tim. *A Passion for Prayer*, Review and Herald Publishing, Hagerstown, MD, 1998.

Finley, Mark. *Light Your World For God,* Hart Books Publishers, Fallbrook, CA. 2002.

_____. *Our Deepest Prayer: Hallowed Be Your Name*, 1-9-11

_____. *Prayer Makes a Difference*, Hart Research Publishers, Fallbrook, CA. 2003.

Froom, Leroy. *Coming of the Comforter*, Review & Herald, Hagerstown, MD, 1956.

Maxwell, John. *Partners in Prayer*, Nelson Books Publishers, Nashville, TN, 1996.

Munroe, Myles Dr. *"Understanding the Purpose and Power of Prayer"* New Kensington, PA: Whitaker House, 2002.

Ogden, Greg. *Discipleship Essentials*, IVP Connect, Downers Grove, Illinois, 2007.

Rugles, Roy. *Teach Us To Pray,* An Instructional Seminar on Prayer.

Sacks, Cheryl. *The Prayer Saturated Church*, Navpress, Colorado Springs, CO, 2004.

Samaan, Philip. *Christ's Way To Pray*, Review and Herald Publishing Association, Hagerstown, MD, 2006.

Shewmaker, Carrol J. *When We Pray For Others*, Review & Harold Publishing, Hagerstown, MD, 1995.

Smith, Dennis. *Spirit Baptism and Prayer*, Tyndale House Publishers, Inc., 2008.

VanderGriend, Alvin. *Praying God's Heart*, PrayerShop Publishing, Terre Haute, IN, 2010.

White, Ellen. *Christ's Object Lessons*, Pacific Press Publishing Association, Washington, D. C., 1941.

_____. *Christ Triumphant*, Review and Herald Publishing Association, Hagerstown, MD, 1999.

_____. *Desires of Ages*, Pacific Press Publishing Association, Nampa, ID, 2002.

_____. *Messages to Young People*, Review and Herald Publishing Association, Hagerstown, MD, 1930.

_____. *Patriarchs and Prophets*, Pacific Press Publishers, Nampa, ID, 2005.

_____. *Prayer*, Pacific Press Publishing Association, Nampa, ID, 2002.

_____. *Prophet and Kings*, Pacific Press Publishing, Nampa, ID, 1917.

_____. *S.D.A. Commentary* Vol. 5, Review & Harold Publishing, Hagerstown, MD, 1956.

_____. *Steps To Christ*, Foy Institute Press, Hagerstown, MD, 1995.

_____. *Testimonies For the Church, Vol. 5*, Pacific Press Publishers, Boise, ID, 1948.

_____. *Testimonies for the Church, Vol. 8*, (Pacific Press Publishing Association, Boise, Idaho, 1948.

_____. *The Acts of the Apostles*, Pacific Press Publishing Association, Nampa, ID, 2005.

_____. *Thoughts From the Mount of Blessing*, Pacific Press Publishing, Boise, Idaho.

Printed in the United States
by Baker & Taylor Publisher Services